Your 60 Minute Lean Business

Just in Time

Your 60 Minute Lean Business
Just in Time
June 2014
First Edition

www.lulu.com
ISBN: 978-1-304-14122-0
Copyright © 2014 Jason Tisbury

All rights reserved. No part of this publication may be reproduced or transmitted in any form or by any means, electronic or mechanical, including photocopying, recording, or by any information storage and retrieval system, without the written permission of the author, except where permitted by law.

Also by Jason Tisbury:

Your 60 Minute Lean Business:
5S Implementation Guide
Total Productive Maintenance
Standardized Work
Kaizen Mindset
Volume 1 – The Foundations

7 Steps To A Lean Business

Contents

Title	Page
Foreword	5
What is Just in Time?	7
Takt Time	9
Load Levelling	14
Theory of Pull Production	20
Kanban	30
Visual Management	40
Putting It All Together	48
Some More Tools	50

Foreword

Welcome to the Your 60 Minute Lean Business series of books. Why 60 minutes? Well for a couple of reasons. It occurred to me a number of years ago while searching through libraries and book stores for texts on the topic of lean manufacturing and lean business that most of the available books were quite large and often not easy to understand for someone new to the topic. The essence of lean is to remove waste from a business and its processes, yet here were all of these books that were filled with non-essential words – waste. I felt a book on the topic of lean should itself be lean. With this in mind I went about writing my first book on lean – 7 Steps To A Lean Business – an overview of lean manufacturing and lean business systems. At 140 pages, this book can be read in a couple of hours and while the details may not enable one to immediately turn a business lean, I believe 7 Steps does provide a very sound overview and ground learning for the lean newcomer.

Now it is time to share the details of some of the different lean tools, I started writing a book detailing all of the tools but soon realised what I was writing wasn't lean enough. And so the 60 Minute Lean Business idea was conceived. Starting with 5S and TPM, the series is now working through the Lean House.

If you are a business owner or manager and are looking for a concise, detailed guide to understanding the benefits of just in time, then this book was written especially for you. My goal is to share what I have been lucky enough to learn with other like minded people who may not have had the dumb luck that I have had. When I say dumb luck, I mean dumb luck. The following is the story of how I came to learn lean, I'm sharing this story to firstly build my credentials and secondly to show how anybody can learn and implement these tools.

At the age of 32 I was working in a factory after a recent business failure when I was lucky enough to break two fingers in a ten ton press. It was quite a bad break, twelve months recovery including two surgeries (one bone graft). Now it may seem strange to call that lucky, but luck is what you make of a situation. Even though I had only one working hand, I could still use a computer, and I was fairly handy on a computer (pun not intended). I ended up working with the Quality Manager who by chance was starting to implement some lean manufacturing / continuous improvement ideas in the business. I learnt a great deal during this time. I was also lucky that this company was in the automotive industry and that one of their main customers was Toyota, probably the best company in the world to learn from. I spent the next five years living and breathing the Toyota Production System (TPS) with direct instruction and mentoring through Toyota. Now after having implemented lean systems and tools through a variety of companies in many organizations in many diverse industries, it is time to share what I have learnt for others to benefit.

What is Just in Time?

Lean Business

Jidoka – Quality

Just In Time

Standardised Work

Kaizen

5S

TPM

Just in time is one of the pillars of the lean house and is a critical element of a lean business. Just in Time (JIT), when deployed correctly will reduce inventory requirements and the cost of poor quality by maintaining a flow of parts/materials in line with the production requirements. This will reduce the impact of many of the 7 wastes:

- Walking
- Overproduction
- Rework
- Motion
- overProcessing
- Inventory
- Transport

There are a number of elements of a successful JIT system. These will be covered in the following chapters:

- Takt Time
- Load levelling
- Theory of production pull
- Kanban systems
- Visual management
- Calculating requirements

1. Takt Time

To understand JIT you must first understand takt time. A common misunderstanding is the belief that takt time has a relationship to or actually is the production cycle time. This is not correct.

Takt time is actually determined from the demand from the customer in relation to the operating hours. In other words the required frequency of each completed part. An often missed component is the relationship to the operating hours or available production time. If the available production time is not an included parameter the flexibility required to achieve takt time will be missing.

So how does takt time differ from cycle time? Let's have a look at what cycle time is and how it is determined.

A production system is generally made up of many smaller processes and pieces of machinery / equipment. Each of these individual processes will have a cycle time that is determined by three main factors:

- Machine auto cycle time
- Manual cycle time
- Load and Unload time

- Changeover time

The process cycle time is the combined time of the above. The total cycle time is the sum of all process cycle times plus any waiting, transport and inventory time.

Now let's have a look at how takt time is calculated.

The most important point to make regarding takt time is that takt time has nothing to do with processing or cycle time. Takt time is often referred to as the 'beat of the customer'.

The formula to calculate takt time is:

T / D

Where:

T = Available Time

D = Customer Demand

Available time is calculated by taking the total operating time, less breaks and planned stoppages, less planned downtime. I like to calculate this based on a single day, however this can be calculated based on a week or month in situations with low demand or availability – more on this later.

For a single day calculation the following formula for available time is used:

Operating hours – total break time = 27360 (sec)

Parallel production streams (full production lines producing same part) = 2

Total planned downtime (includes both production lines) = 2700 (sec)

27360 x 2 - 2700 = 52020

In the above example the operating day is 8.5 hours and has an unpaid 30 minute lunch break and 24 minutes of other paid breaks throughout the day. This leaves an effective work day of 7.6 hours or 7 hours and 36 minutes. The facility has two productions lines producing the same part; these lines are independent of each other and share no machinery or process steps. There is also planned downtime of 45 minutes on one of the lines on this day.

Let's say the customer demand is 600 units per day for this example. When we apply the takt time formula from the previous page – 52020 / 600 – 86.7. Our takt time on this day is 87.6 seconds; this means a part needs to be completed every 87.6 seconds to keep up with customer demand. If we produce faster than this we will over produce and create inventory. Overproduction is the worst of the seven wastes as it contributes to all of the other wastes. If we produce slower than 87.6 seconds we will not meet the customers demand and will have to deploy overtime or rely on inventory produced earlier; both of these are wastes of sorts.

This is where the difference between takt time and cycle time is important to understand. The total or overall cycle time is technically irrelevant, what is important is the individual process cycle times in comparison to the takt time; this will be discussed in greater detail in the next chapter.

By concerning ourselves with and measuring performance against takt time we are thinking about the customers requirements; we are not constrained in our thinking by what we believe are the best possible cycle times. By focusing on meeting the customer demand we open opportunities for innovation and continuous improvement.

Because the takt time is calculated from the demand and the available time, the takt time can vary from day to day and can vary significantly throughout months and years. Both of the factors in the formula are variables. The production system needs to be flexible an agile enough to respond to changes in demand and available time (often due to planned / unplanned downtime). Steps and solutions to help achieve this flexibility are contained in the following pages and in other titles in the Your 60 Minute Lean Business series. Having a robust demand planning system is one solution that can be effective. This enables the production to be leveled across a period of time rather than relying solely on leveling production and workloads through the production process alone. Demand planning does have inherent risks of creating inventory if not effectively managed.

2. Load Leveling

The term load leveling can apply to many different aspects of business. In the context of this book we will be discussing load leveling on two fronts. The first will be analyzing takt time and cycle time with a view to balancing and the second will be machine and operator load leveling to eliminate overburden and underutilization. Separately these two areas of change can significantly improve your efficiencies; together they will have an even greater impact and enable you to meet your customer's requirements in a cost effective manner. Load leveling is often referred to as heijunka – this is a Japanese term and methodology which is used in Toyota Production System (TPS).

Takt Time vs Cycle Time

It is important to compare the cycle times of the machines used in your production streams against the required takt time. Just in time is all about eliminating the wastes of manufacturing, particularly over production as this will result in inventory, transportation, rework and possibly over processing; if you have machine cycle times that are greater than the takt time you will have to put in place solutions. This analysis will provide the information necessary to make informed decisions.

To simplify the explanation we'll use an example based on a fictional production line scenario. The parameters of the scenario are as follows:

Takt time – 94 seconds

Machine cycle times:

1. 44 seconds
2. 62 seconds
3. 65 seconds
4. 105 seconds
5. 57 seconds
6. 96 seconds

The first step has already been completed as we know the takt time and we have measured the machine cycle times. The next step is to chart the measurements.

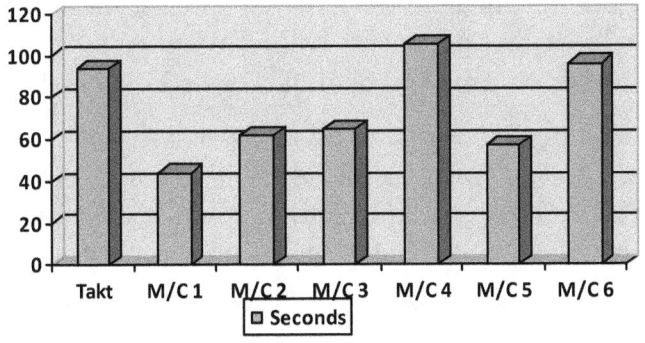

By charting the results of the measurement analysis it can be clearly visualized which machines operate outside of the takt time. These are machines four and six. It is also clear the imbalance between the machines used in this process; the difference between the shortest and longest machine time is over double. This will make it difficult to balance the production line.

If all of the machines in the above example were to run at their capacity we would see a buildup of stock between machines 1 and 2, 2 and 3, 3 and 4 and 5 and 6. If this is a single piece flow production line we would have machine 5 waiting for the completion of machine 4 and due to machines 4 and 6 cycle times being greater than the takt time we would not meet customer demand.

So what are the options available to us to solve this problem? There are at least four options:

1) Produce finished product to the longest cycle time and fail to achieve takt time. This will result in a failure to supply the customer on time and could lead to a loss of sales.

2) Have all machines operating at capacity (cycle time). This will result in inventory as discussed in the above paragraph and will still result in a failure to supply the customer. Once again, this could lead to a loss of customers and sales.

3) Kaizen the machinery to reduce the variance in cycle times across the line. This can achieve some improvement, however with the variance so great between M/C 1 and

M/C 4 this approach is likely to prove challenging and probably quite expensive.

4) Build stock of finished product ahead of schedule. This will enable supply to customer demand when stock levels are managed, however will result in higher inventory levels which in turn can lead to rework. It is likely that cash flow would also be impacted by this practice.

5) Build to kanban (discussed in chapter 4) or determined stock levels for each step. This will eliminate or reduce the impacts of the issues identified in option 4; however customer demand will not be met unless some machine kaizen is successfully undertaken on machines 4 and 6.

OPERATOR LOAD LEVELLING

This is similar to the above discussion, however we are focusing now on operators rather than machines. There are two reasons for us to analyse the operator loads.

1) To ensure takt time can be achieved

2) To ensure operator workloads are equalized to avoid overburden and / or underutilisation.

The problems with overburdening operators are many and include:

- Increased likelihood of OHS issues arising; this is both from overuse injury and hazards / injuries caused by fatigue.
- Increased likelihood of poor quality resulting from fatigue and / or rushing through the workload
- Poor productivity

Problems arising from underutilisation are similar in result with increased likelihood of OHS issues and quality problems. In the case of underutilisation however these are caused by inactivity which reduces a persons awareness.

Uneven workloads can lead to morale issues amongst the work teams. Poor morale is one on the great negative forces in any business. Morale is not only a good indicator of an organisations management; it is also a barrier to success or a precursor to failure.

The best tool to balance the operator workload is through standardised work. Your 60 Minute Lean Business – Standardised Work is available in paperback and ebook.

YAMAZUMI CHART

A Yamazumi chart is a stacked chart used to show the steps within a process and the breakdown of work type. These work types are Value Adding, Incidental and Waste. As the objective of lean is to identify and eliminate waste in the value stream, a Yamazumi chart is a valuable tool.

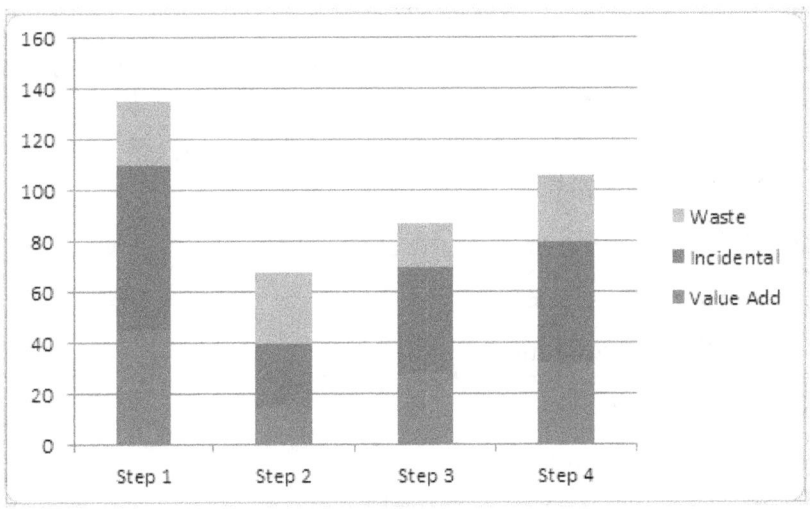

The above example shows how a Yamazumi chart breaks down the three work types. It is clearly shown in the example that value added work makes up less than a third of the total cycle time. A standard spreadsheet application can be used to develop the charts.

3. Theory of Pull Productionl

Before discussing pull production, let's look at the traditional push method of production flow.

Push Production

With traditional push production flow the product is "pushed" through the production process. If we look at a general manufacturing business the following high level flow may occur:

1) Sales order received

2) Job planned for manufacture

3) Materials purchased

4) Production scheduled

5) Materials received

6) Materials into inventory

7) Production schedule received by production

8) Raw materials enter production

9) First processing step completed

10) Part finished product to inventory or waiting

11) Second process step scheduled

12) Parts collected / delivered to second process step

13) Second process step completed
14) Finished part into inventory
15) Sales order opened
16) Picking slip raised
17) Product picked
18) Product invoiced
19) Product shipped to customer

The above is a very simple two process manufacturing value stream and look at how many steps are involved. Also note there are four inventory steps. Whenever we have inventory, we add cost, risk safety and quality and impact efficiency.

If we were to develop a current state value stream map of such a model we would see something similar to the below diagram. Note the high amount of non-value added time in inventory and the high dependency on Planning to co-ordinate the pulling of product from inventory and processing. Just over one percent of the lead time is actually processing time; the balance is waiting in inventory in this example. Many businesses are not much better placed than this believe it or not.

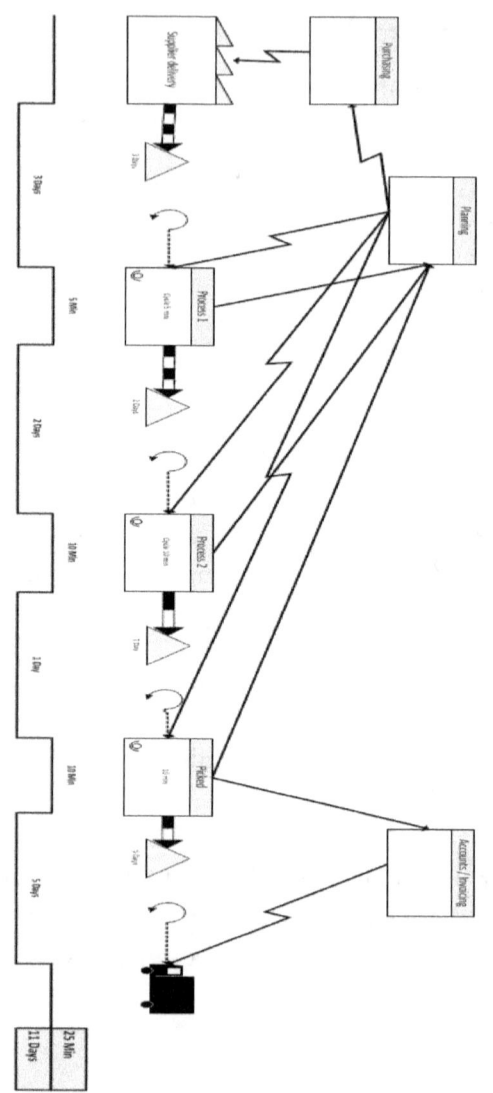

The below diagram illustrates how a conventional push production system operates. Notice the involvement of planning all through the production process. This involvement may by large or small, however it is always present when a push method is practiced.

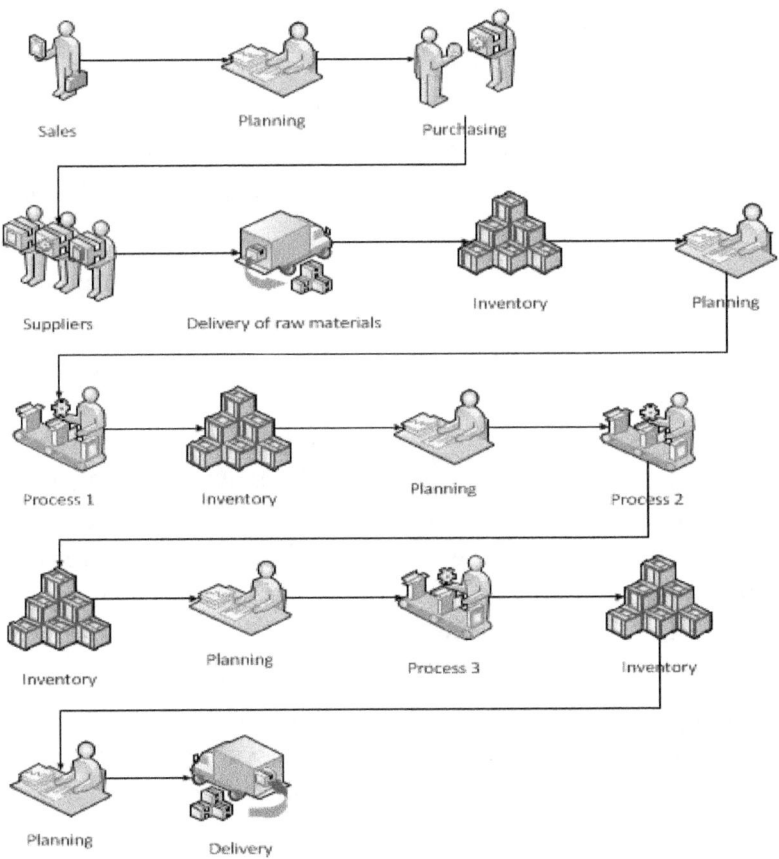

As you can see from the above illustration of a simple three stage manufacturing business, the processes can become quite long winded and very dependent on support services. For example, planning is involved five times in the above example. There are also four inventory stages; every time we have inventory, we are tying up capital.

To summarise the push method, we have a lot of inventory, waiting and interaction with planning/production control. The high level of interaction with planning and production control may not seem too big an issue however every time this interaction takes place resources are taken away from adding value to the product. Any excessive interaction is waste.

Pull Production

By contrast, pull production occurs almost in reverse by principle. Rather than the primary instruction going to the first process step, in a perfect pull production system, an instruction to dispatch will be provided to the warehouse. This instruction will start a series of instructions backwards through the process flow. The warehouse will request a completed part from the final process step or take from a supermarket which will trigger the completion of a part. The below diagram illustrates how a pull system works; notice the differences from the conventional push system.

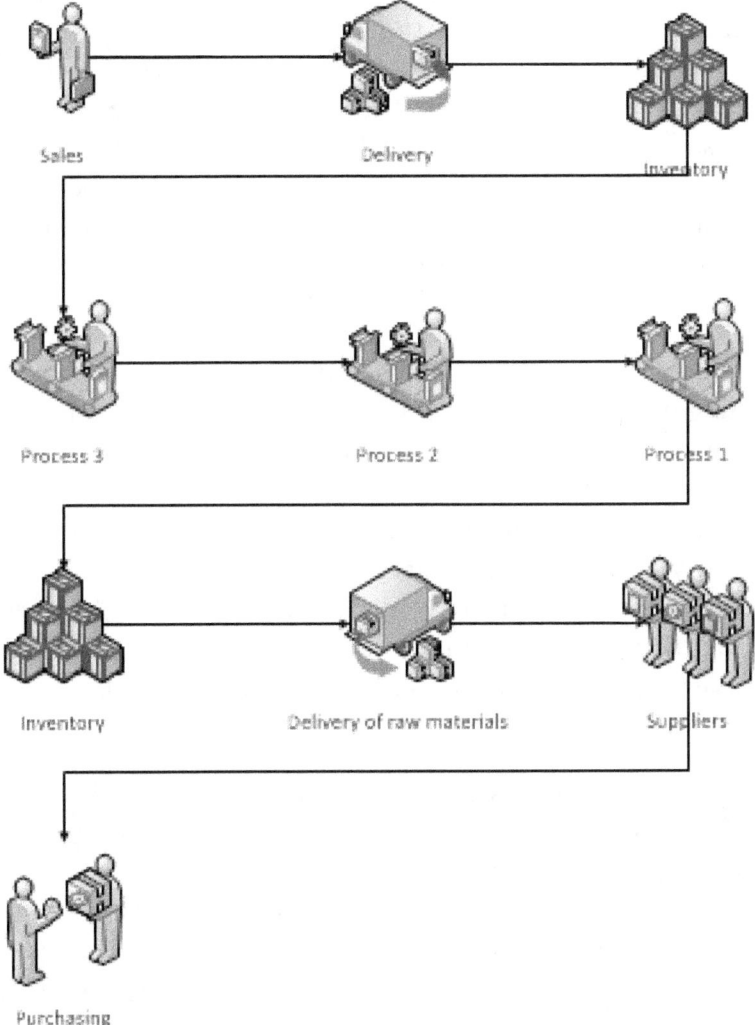

As you can see, the primary instruction to manufacture is to the final manufacturing process. There are a number of keys to an effective pull production system. Kanban is the trigger system used to initiate production at each step and is discussed in detail in the next chapter; visual management is used to clearly communicate the status of the systems and is discussed in Chapter 5; a leveled production process and matched inventory system are also keys. Leveled production was discussed in Chapter 2, now we will begin to understand why it is important.

The major keys to an effective pull production system are defining where in the process to hold inventory to maximize JIT and minimize cost of inventory and how much inventory to carry. Even a perfect one piece flow system requires some inventory of components. As we all know inventory is one the seven wastes; therefore we require any inventory to be measured and managed. Every business, product and system is unique so a flat rule cannot be given, however there are some guidelines that can be used.

> 1) At what points in the production process does the raw material become a "product"? In every process there is a point where we go from stocking components to assemblies, this point in the process is important to identify. Some organisations setup their bills of material at these point to call them sub-assemblies or "child parts". It is often at these points that supermarkets can be setup. It is also at these points that the sub-assemblies may be commonly used in a variety of

assemblies or "parent parts". Thus providing more than one single demand point for the sub-assemblies in the supermarket

2) How many parent parts create demand for the sub-assemblies? The greater the number of parent parts creating demand reduces the risk of dead inventory.

3) What is the averaged, peak and low demand for the sub-assembly? If demand is not constant or stable for this subassembly then a supermarket may create more waste (inventory).

4) What is the total processing time to manufacture to the sub-assembly stage? If the processing time to this stage is greater than takt time then extra shifts or other alternatives may be required with a supermarket setup to hold inventory.

5) Is the production line used for any other products or is it stand alone? If a line is multipurpose, the availability of resources (man and machine) will be limited compared to a standalone line where the manpower can be utilized elsewhere and the machinery left idle.

The below VSM diagram shows the same process used in the push production example, however now in a pull production method. Note, there has been no kaizen or standardized work applied so the cycle times and inventory are the same.

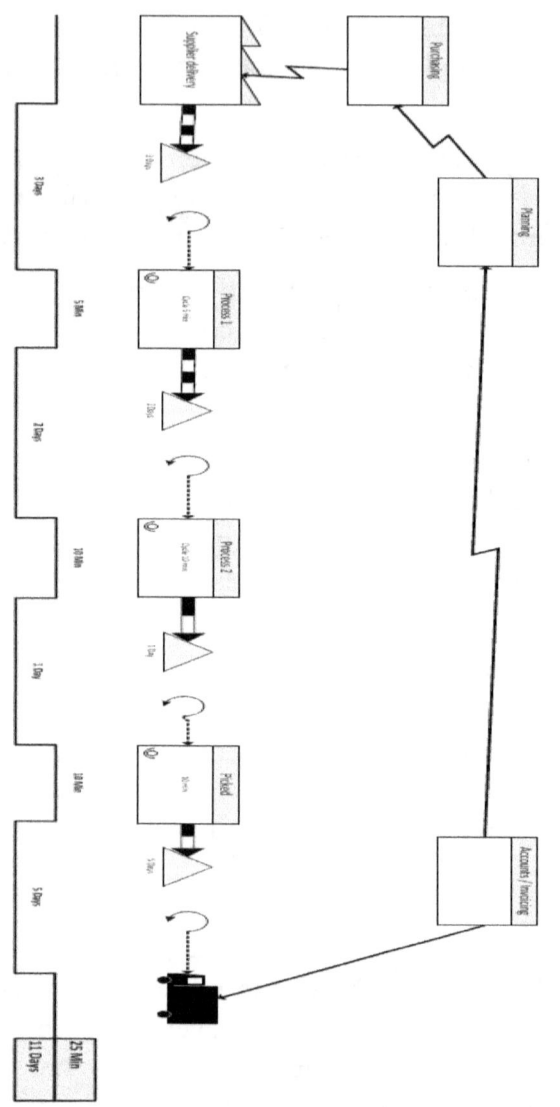

As you can see, even without improvements to the processes, the communication has been greatly reduced by implementing a Pull Methodology. Alone, this reduction in communication requirements will:

- Reduce resource requirements for administration

- Reduce / eliminate errors brought about by incorrect communications

The true benefits of pull production are realised through the reduction of inventory throughout the processing. Because each process step is producing to the demand of the next step (or supermarket requirement; it must be said here that a supermarket doesn't have to hold a large inventory, it can hold a single item) overproduction will not occur. To manage a pull production system, there needs to be a trigger to produce at each step; the best system to manage this is through the use of kanban.

4. Kanban

The term kanban comes directly from the Toyota Production System and literally means 'board'. Often, kanban is incorrectly described as a material management system; kanban is simply a system used to trigger an activity (this could be production, material movement or shipment).

Kanban can take many different forms, however the most common is a card system which will be used for the following explanation before providing details of some other common systems.

Kanban Card

The simple kanban card is probably the most common type of kanban used. The card can take many forms, however usually contains the following information:

- Part / Inventory Number
- Part / Inventory Name
- Short description
- Image of component
- Kanban type
- Supplier

- Qty on Kanban
- Lead time
- Item location
- Card / Kanban Number of
- Responsible planner / buyer

The Kanban system is a replenishment system used in place of a materials requirement planning (MRP) system. The two systems are not intended to be used for the same parts. This is where many businesses come unstuck; they use a kanban system and continue to use their MRP system. This creates confusion and / or complacency. A card system works by triggering the supplier (this can be internal or external) to produce a part or quantity of parts. It really can be that simple. Some businesses choose to maintain an internal only kanban system; in these instances the trigger is often used to initiate the purchasing process from a supplier. While not as effective in reducing waste as a supplier kanban, this model can still provide good benefits.

A simple internal kanban process between a warehouse and production is defined in the following diagram.

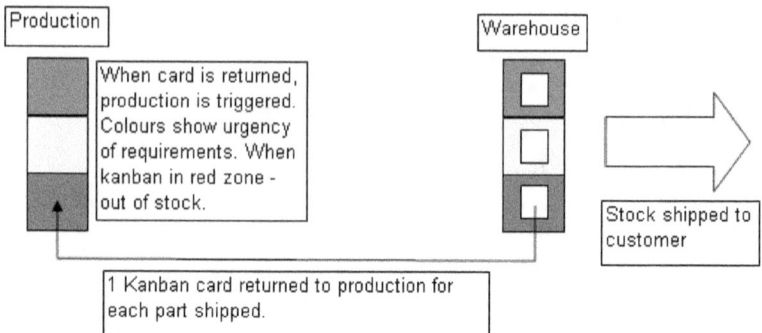

The kanban is triggered by the shipment of a part to the customer. In classic pull production theory this action creates demand on production to produce a part. The kanban card is returned to production as a trigger to fill the demand. When the part is completed it is returned to the warehouse with the kanban card. The colour-coding is used to visually display the urgency. When the first card is returned to production both the warehouse staff and production staff can easily see there is a demand, however as there is still stock available in the warehouse (in this case two) the replacement can be made with normal priority. If the second card is returned to production it is clear there is now some urgency as stock is now low. When the third card is returned to production, the warehouse is now out of stock and replacements should be expedited. There is some science behind the volumes which will be explained in further detail in a later section.

In the above example, two simple three position kanban boards are used – one in the warehouse and another in production. A single card is stored in each position meaning the inventory of finished goods will not exceed three units. For a low volume selling item this may be okay, for larger volume items there are a couple of options.

1) Increase the number of pegs and cards to increase the total size of inventory.

2) Store multiple cards on each peg. Once again this will increase the total size of inventory.

Of these two options the first offers greater visibility and control of inventory. A simple system as above can be effective for high or low volume parts and can be used throughout the value stream to trigger staged production, materials, and even resource planning. Kanban will work in small, medium or large organisations and can be effectively implemented without expensive infrastructure or technology.

A card kanban system does require resources to monitor and collect cards; this is often tasked to material handlers on a material route. It is also important to highlight the need to manage the kanban system. Just like any other system there is an element of management and maintenance required for the system to consistently operate at its optimum level. This maintenance may be required for a number of reasons including:

- Changes in demand

- Changes in design or specification
- Changes in supplier
- Lost or damaged cards

Bin System Kanban

Another common type of Kanban system is the Bin System. While the concept of a trigger is the same as with the Kanban card, a bin system is used in place of the cards and visual boards. There are two main variations to the Bin System; Two Bin and Three Bin.

Two Bin System

As the name implies this is a system comprising of two bins; one at the user and the other in the process of replenishment. A two bin system can be useful where demand is low and parts are complex so a minimum level of inventory provides significant cost benefits.

Three Bin System

Similar to the two bin system, this system utilizes three bins and is the more common of the bin type Kanban systems in use. Once again, one bin will be at the user, one at the supplier being replenished and in this instance the third will be in transit to the user or in transit to the supplier. The benefit of this system over the two bin system is the faster replenishment to the user when the replenishment is triggered. Whereas the two bin system where the trigger to replenish comes when the first bin is empty or returned creating a gap in supply as the full bin from the supplier is transported, the third bin is constantly in transit or awaiting internal movement to the work area. This does increase the total inventory or WIP within the system as there are now three bins rather than two.

Although there are some different methods to manage the replenishment the basics of kanban remain. A signal is used to trigger the replenishment method. Whether you use the cards and visual board, a bin system, a combination or any other method the basic principles are the same.

Many organizations struggle through the implementation of kanban due to a misconception that once implemented, a kanban system no longer requires management. Just like any other system, it will require monitoring, measurement and management as discussed earlier. This is an important concept to understand; resources must be made available. Another reason businesses struggle is the lack of planning and understanding of the system setup.

Kanban System Setup

For any system there are certain requirements that will ensure the optimum results. With kanban these requirements are largely the calculations as discussed below.

As in everything else, there are almost as many formulae for kanban calculations as there are lines of inventory. I am a believer in keeping things simple, so with this approach I give you the simple kanban calculation.

$$\frac{\text{Daily Demand} \times \text{Lead Time (Days)} \times \text{Safety Factor}}{\text{Container Size}}$$

Daily demand is simply the average daily usage of the part. If you use the item sporadically, take a total over a month or even quarter and divide by the number of days to determine the daily demand.

Lead time is the time taken for delivery (from either internal or external supplier) from the day the kanban is triggered until physical parts are available on line for use. This is measured in days to enable easy calculation with daily demand.

The safety factor is a measure of your confidence in your systems, processes and suppliers. The standard is 1; if you have very low confidence this may be a 2. In between 1 and 2 provides the levels of confidence.

Container size is the number of parts in each container. This may be 1 or as high as you like. This enables you to talk in containers rather than total quantity of parts.

To give the formula some substance here it is again with some data around it:

Daily Demand = 25 units
Lead Time = 5 days
Safety Factor = 1
Container Size = 25

For the above data, the formula would look like this:

$$\frac{25 \times 5 \times 1}{25}$$

The result would be 5 containers or 125 units. This is the total amount of parts within the kanban system for this particular part. Where these are situated within the system is negotiated between you and the supplier. They will be either;

1) In your store
2) At your supplier
3) In transit
4) At a 3rd party

We can change the data used to make in more interesting:

Daily Demand = 30 units
Lead Time = 3 days
Safety Factor = 1.4
Container size = 15

$$\frac{30 \times 3 \times 1.4}{15}$$

This results in 8.4 containers or 126 units; we will round-up the containers to the next whole one. Never round-down! This will result in 9 containers or 135 units in the system. As we work with the supplier and gain more confidence in their performance the safety factor can reduce which will result in a reduction of the total quantity to a minimum of 6 containers or 90 units (3 days inventory). Remember, this inventory is not all within your system as roughly 1/3 will be in process with your supplier, 1/3 in transit and 1/3 in stock.

I have intentionally used a simple formula to both aide comprehension and simplify the explanations. I use the same formula in every business I work with and have for more than ten years. There are many more complex formulae used by many practitioners and I'm sure some do have some benefits however in my experience the more complex the system, the more problems will be met along your journey.

A kanban system should be easy to use, easy to determine when it is working on track and even easier to determine when it is off track! That is the beauty of kanban, you shouldn't need a PhD to setup the system or use the system. An effective system can be setup and managed by just about anyone and everyone in the business should be able to determine whether there is a problem or not.

After setting up and running your kanban system you may find there are some issues with either excess inventory or out of stock. Don't panic and throw out the system. This just means your calculations are a little (or a lot) off. As you gain experience in setting up kanban systems you will reduce these errors; remember though, the kanban system isn't a set and leave system. It is a dynamic system that will require updates in line with demand, product changes and supplier performance.

5. Visual Management

Visual management is a very general term and plays a significant role in lean organisations. In this chapter, we will discuss firstly visual management in general, followed by visual management specifically for JIT management.

General Visual Management

Visual management is all around us. We see it in the supermarkets, when driving, when watching television. In today's society it really is everywhere. How do you know where to purchase the fuel for your car? Visual management! All of the service stations display their prices and the benefits of making your purchase with them; you select the one that best suits your needs. This is visual management.

When embarking on a flying holiday, how do you know where to find the airport? Visual management!

Have you ever noticed how difficult some cities are to navigate? The easier ones have clear relevant signage that don't rely on words alone. Once again this is visual management.

I think you get the message; visual management is all around us, in all parts of our life. The key to effective visual management is to clearly communicate with as little complexity as possible.

Let's look at some examples of general visual management.

1) The below sign is so simple. It contains both words in English and a universal symbol meaning do not enter.

2) Another classic simple sign. This time First Aid.

3) Once again we have symbols to assist in the comprehension of these common signs. Note the use of colours – red to denote prohibited.

4) The No Smoking sign doesn't even use words to get its point across.

In all of the above examples, the use of images or symbols helps the sharing of the information. In none of these instances do the communicators rely on words alone to get their message across. Very simple strategy; the challenge is to make this work for other types of communication.

Now let's discuss some visual management used in some other areas. The world of marketing is often overlooked when discussing effective visual management, I believe they provide some valuable lessons. What are the most recognizable images I around the globe? MacDonald's and Coca-Cola; all around the world when these logos are displayed most of the population will know exactly what they are. Yes, they are marketed extensively and effectively however it is nothing more than very effective visual management.

Visual Management in the workplace

In the business environment, visual management is used to communicate many things including:
- OHS information
- Company policies
- General communications
- 5S storyboards and audit boards
- Standardized work instructions

The list really does go on and on, one of the best uses of visual management is for Just in Time and especially kanban.

For JIT, visual management can be used to communicate the standard work used to control the materials handling. Just like for a manufacturing or office process where standardized work is used, it should be used for the delivery and distribution of the materials. This standardized work will include the material handler's route, frequency and inventory count and will be tied in with the process standardized work and takt time. This visual management can be in the form of central boards or displays and / or on the material handling trolley (if in use). If displayed centrally, this will have two benefits:

1) The material handler/s will have a backup location for their route and timings.

2) The work of the material handler/s will be openly distributed and communicated. This will result in easy auditing of the work and a broad understanding of the route. This will reduce the amount of chasing up by other departments.

Visual management in the warehouse for JIT can be as simple as labelling of racking, locations and inventory to min/max levels, restocking timings and Kanban boards. It can also be used in a similar way for line-side stocking where a conventional warehouse is not used or is the supplier to the line-side primary locations.

We discussed the Kanban Board earlier in this book, the kanban board is a form of visual management. Kanban is often linked closely with a manufacturing or warehousing environment as this is where the concept originated. Many people don't realize kanban can be used just as effectively in the office, service and IT environments. As the name kanban mean "trigger" it can be used to trigger any activity; kanban is a perfect system to use for project management. This use of visual management is still JIT as we are using the visual management to trigger the next steps of a business process.

6. Pulling it all together

So far we have looked at the theories of takt time; load levelling; pull production; Kanban and visual management. Now let's look at how all of this comes together to give us a Just in Time system. The best way to explain how this all works is to work backwards through what we have learnt so far.

In the context of JIT, visual management is the method used to communicate the process and the status of the process. It is also used to train, audit and review the process. Without visual management would the JIT system still work? In some instances it would still work however it never will be as effective. To say visual management is just the communication of the system is selling it a fair bit short as it is an integrated part of a sustainable system.

Kanban is a control method, just as many organisations use a Materials Resource Planning (MRP) system, others use Kanban to control the ordering, supply and distribution of materials, part finished and finished product. Some organisations even try a combination of MRP and kanban with varying results. As neither of these systems are developed to be run with the other it can be challenging to get good results from this combined method. I have seen a couple of organisations pull it off with some success however I'm not convinced this is the right approach due to the amount of controls and management required to ensure both systems are running in alignment. A better approach is to use the kanban system to manage the supply, delivery and distribution and use the accounting side of the MRP system only to capture and record the transactions. While the best MRP systems can be effective in managing the supply chain, an easy and effective kanban system will reduce the amount of system support and system management required.

While kanban is a method used to control a JIT system, pull production is at the heart of JIT. Pull production is both the driving force and the end result of a JIT system. With a pull production system you are reversing the traditional ideas of batch processing. Understanding the concept of pull production is absolutely critical to the success of a JIT system. With the traditional push method of production, each process produces as fast as it can and builds up stock at the output side of the process. This stock is transported to either inventory or the next process step when scheduled. Each process produces independent of the other processes with little or no consideration of inventory levels other than the scheduling or planning system. With a push system you are relying heavily on the scheduling and planning to be of a high standard; this does make the production system less nimble to changes as the lead times can be longer. In contrast, a JIT system can be more nimble due to the reduced inventory levels and reduced involvement required from scheduling and planning. A pull system empowers the production team to reduce inventory levels and achieve greater true efficiency through production of customer requirements only (not making to stock).

Whereas the last three stages are the process, controls and communication, load levelling is one of the requirements of a JIT system. This is because for a JIT system to be effective and sustainable it is important to have the material flowing efficiently through the processes with little or no impact by bottlenecks. To achieve this, the line must be balanced, otherwise the bottlenecks will stop the flow and create pockets of high and low inventory. Whenever inventory pockets show up they must be managed; this can be achieved through a supermarket to feed a process after a low inventory process or to capture before a bottleneck. Supermarkets are a commonly used control when line balancing cannot be achieved. It needs to be understood though, that whenever a supermarket is used your inventory levels are increasing and this will impact cashflow as well as introduce the risks associated with over-production. These risks include:

- Rework or scrap due to changes in design or obsoletion

- Excessive transportation and movement of stock

- Safety risks associated with the above

The challenge is to identify the opportunities to level the load without falling into the trap of too many supermarkets. The supermarket is an easy option, however should be used as the last resort or when the return on investment in the quest for levelling cannot be justified.

This brings us to takt time, the heartbeat of the customer. Without understanding the takt time the next steps would be impossible to do effectively. Remember, takt time is simply the available work time divided by the customer demand and tells you the required frequency for finished product. Understanding takt time is the key to your sustainable success with a JIT supply chain and broader lean business system.

7. Some more tools

This chapter contains a couple of useful tools that can be used to assist a business in achieving and maintaining an effective JIT system. The tools in this section are not prerequisites or 'must haves', however can be of great benefit and assistance in the overall lean system.

Tool 1) Quick change over

Quick change over (QCO) has a couple of alternative names:

 - Quick Die Change Over (QDCO)
 - Single Minute Exchange of Dies (SMED)

The reason I have removed the reference to Dies in the title is to maintain a relevance in the greater business environment. In today's world, most businesses do not use dies in their process; even if they are in manufacturing. Just because a business doesn't use dies doesn't mean they don't have change overs. Even in an office or administration environment there are changeover processes that occur. The ability to changeover in a shorter amount of time than a competitor can save you money and give you a genuine competitive advantage in the market. How do you calculate your changeover time?

The total time from last completed (good) part to the completion of the next completed (good) part is defined as the changeover time. A good part is defined as a usable part that meets the correct specifications and can be a manufactured part, an engineered part or even a document. The changeover time is broken down into two parts:

- External time / elements
- Internal time / elements

External time consists work elements that can be performed while the last part and / or first part are being produced. External components can only be achieved where there are automated processes within the work elements (not changeover elements) or by another operator / resource. With automated processes the operator is free to prepare for, begin or complete the changeover process while the last and / or first parts are being produced.

Internal time consists of all work elements that are performed while no parts are being produced. This is similar in definition to incidental work time in that the internal changeover work elements must be performed to enable production to commence, however the time taken to perform these functions takes away from the value adding time.

The target of QCO is to reduce (or as much as possible eliminate) the internal time / elements of the changeover to increase the value add time. This is done by following the Standardized Work methodology however instead of measuring and improving the processing elements you are measuring the elements of the changeover. A more thorough instruction can be found in the book 'Your 60 Minute Lean Business – Standardized Work'; but here is a quick overview of how to implement the Standardized Work method for changeovers:

1) First measure the entire changeover time from last good part to first good part. If possible measure multiple changeovers to understand the repeatable time and any common issues identified across the multiple examples.

2) Measure the changeover again, this time taking note of the element steps of the changeover. Make sure you record whether the steps are internal or external. Once again, multiple recordings are recommended wherever possible.

3) Calculate the total internal and external time separately, to indicate where the waste in the process is contained.

4) Analyse the internal changeover elements. These should be reduced or eliminated first as these elements are performed when the process has stopped and is true waste. Remember the customer only pays for the value added processes.

5) When the internal element improvements have been exhausted (at least those prioritized with good return on investment or ROI) you can analyze the external elements

to identify opportunities. Improvements in the external elements will not achieve a reduction in overall changeover time or waste, however can result in other efficiency gains by freeing up labour resources for other activities.

By reducing the changeover times in your business you can achieve greater line balancing and reduce the requirement for inventory between processing steps and achieve improved JIT performance.

Dedicated material handlers

An area many businesses fail to resource in the drive toward a lean business is that of materials handling. Unfortunately many quickly forget the real objective of lean and simply (and incorrectly) believe lean is 'doing more with less'. This approach can lead to failure. Lean is about doing more with the right resources. Under resourcing can lead to just as much waste as over resourcing. Effective material handling resources are imperative to achieving a sustainable and effective JIT system. So how do you know if you have the right amount of resources?

First, we need to look at what these resources might be. Obviously, a business can employ manual handlers to undertake the material movement throughout the business. Many businesses utilize technology for the material handling and with the costs and associated management systems of robotics becoming less and less this is becoming more accessible to a broader type of business. This technology can be as simple as conveyors to as hi-tech as automated robots delivering on a standardized route.

Once you have determined the type of material handling resources it is necessary to determine the resource requirements. This must come after the JIT standardized work has been defined as these calculations will determine the number of resources. Just as we work to balance the work on a production line, we should work to balance the load for the material handlers. A simple Yamazumi chart measured against takt time will enable these calculations to be effective.

www.ingramcontent.com/pod-product-compliance
Lightning Source LLC
Chambersburg PA
CBHW072253170526
45158CB00003BA/1069